What Kind of Animal Is It?

Dolphins and Other Marine Mammals

Kelley MacAulay & Bobbie Kalman

A Crabtree Crown Book

Crabtree Publishing
crabtreebooks.com

Dolphins and Other Marine Mammals

Editor-in-chief
Bobbie Kalman

Writing team
Kelley MacAulay
Bobbie Kalman

Substantive editor
Kathryn Smithyman

Editors
Molly Aloian
Reagan Miller

Design
Margaret Salter

Consultant
Patricia Loesche, Ph.D., Animal Behavior Program, Department of Psychology, University of Washington

Production manager
Candice Campbell

Images
Shutterstock.com

Crabtree Publishing

crabtreebooks.com 800-387-7650

In Canada: We acknowledge the financial support of the Government of Canada through the Canada Book Fund for our publishing activities.

Printed in the U.S.A./CP032026

Published in Canada
Crabtree Publishing
616 Welland Ave.
St. Catharines,
Ontario L2M 5V6

Published in the United States
Crabtree Publishing
347 Fifth Ave.
Suite 1402-145
New York, NY 10016

Hardcover: 978-1-0398-7316-2
Paperback: 978-1-0398-7374-2
Ebook (pdf): 978-1-0398-7423-7
Epub: 978-1-0398-7472-5

Library and Archives Canada Cataloguing in Publication
Available at Library and Archives Canada

Library of Congress Cataloging-in-Publication Data
Available at the Library of Congress

Contents

Many marine mammals

dolphin

porpoise

Marine mammals are animals that live mainly in oceans. Every kind of marine mammal belongs to a group. There are five different groups of marine mammals. The groups are shown on these pages.

whale

1. Dolphins, whales, and porpoises make up one group of marine mammals.

2. Sea otters form their own group of marine mammals.

What is a mammal?

Mammals are animals that

- have hair or fur on their bodies
- breathe air using **lungs** (See page 8.)
- are **warm-blooded** (See page 10.)
- have **backbones** (See page 12.)
- **nurse** when they are young (See page 14.)

dugong

manatee

3. Dugongs and manatees make up a group of marine mammals.

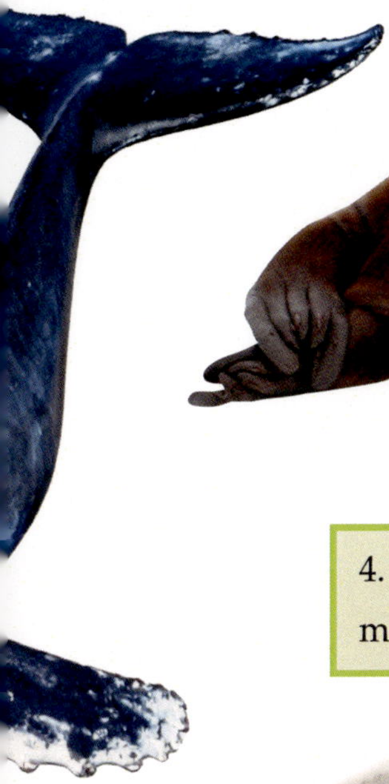

walrus

sea lion

4. Another group of marine mammals is made up of walruses, sea lions, and seals.

seal

polar bear

5. Polar bears form their own group of marine mammals.

In water, on land

Some marine mammals live in water all the time. Most live in ocean **habitats**. A habitat is the natural place where an animal lives. Some marine mammals live in deep, cold ocean waters. Others live in warm, shallow waters close to land. A few types of marine mammals live in rivers.

Most manatees live in warm, shallow parts of oceans. Some live in rivers.

These dolphins are called common dolphins. They live in the deep parts of oceans.

Two habitats

A few kinds of marine mammals live both in water and on land. Some live mainly in oceans, but they spend time on land. Others live mainly on land, but they spend time in oceans.

Sea lions live mainly in oceans. They sometimes rest on land. The sea lion shown right is resting on a sandy beach.

Polar bears live in cold places. They live mainly on ice and snowy lands. They spend some time swimming in oceans.

Breathing air

Marine mammals must breathe air to stay alive. They breathe air using lungs. Dolphins, whales, and porpoises have **blowholes** that let air into their lungs. A blowhole is a hole on top of an animal's head. The animals lift their blowholes above water to breathe in or blow out air.

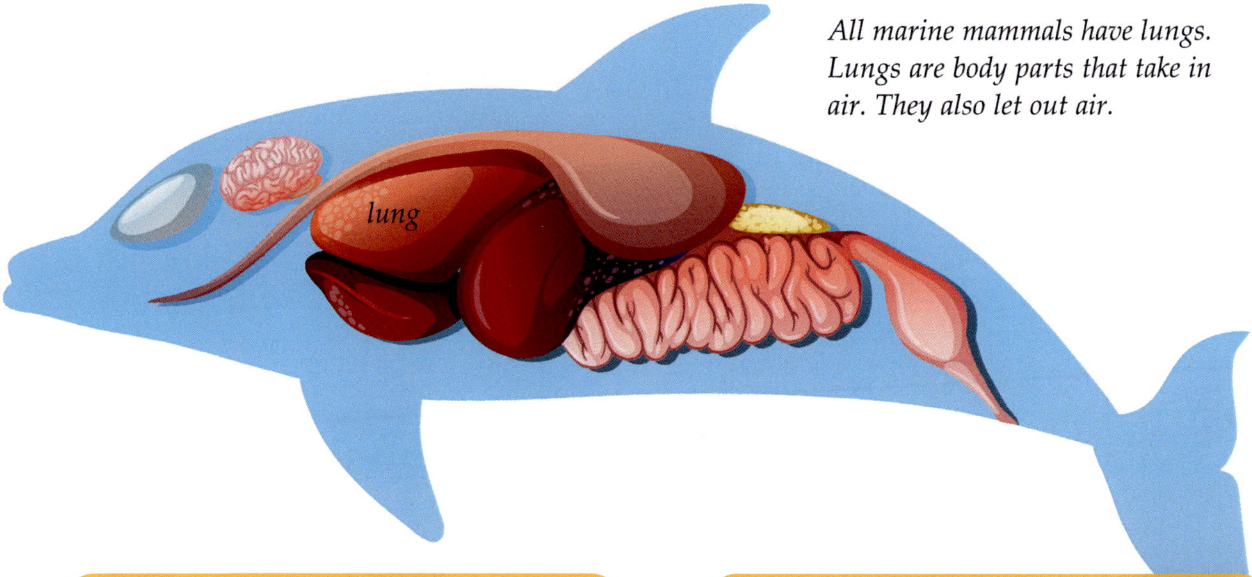

All marine mammals have lungs. Lungs are body parts that take in air. They also let out air.

A dolphin swims to the surface to breathe. The dolphin's blowhole opens to let in air. When the dolphin goes back under water, its blowhole closes.

Nostril breathing

Some marine mammals do not have blowholes. These animals breathe air through their mouths or **nostrils**. When the animals are swimming, they lift their heads above water to take breaths of air.

This seal is taking a breath of air through its nostrils. Seals that live in cold places must find holes in the ice for breathing. They stick their heads up through these holes.

Warm blood

A walrus has thick rolls of blubber on its body.

A marine mammal is a warm-blooded animal. The body temperature of a warm-blooded animal always stays about the same. It does not matter if the animal is in a warm place or a cold place. A marine mammal has thick layers of fat on its body to help keep it warm in cold water. This fat is called **blubber**.

Warm fur

Some marine mammals have thick fur covering their bodies. Having fur on their bodies helps keep the animals warm. Other marine mammals do not have fur on their bodies. They may have a few whiskers around their noses.

Baby dolphins have a few whiskers when they are born. Adult dolphins have no whiskers.

Sea otters have both warm fur and whiskers on their bodies.

Strong bodies

Most marine mammals have strong bodies that are built for swimming. Their bodies are smooth and sleek. Smooth, sleek bodies glide easily and quickly through water.

Dolphins, whales, and porpoises have ***tail flukes****. Tail flukes help these animals swim through water.*

Bodies with backbones

Marine mammals have backbones inside their bodies. A backbone is a group of bones in the middle of an animal's back.

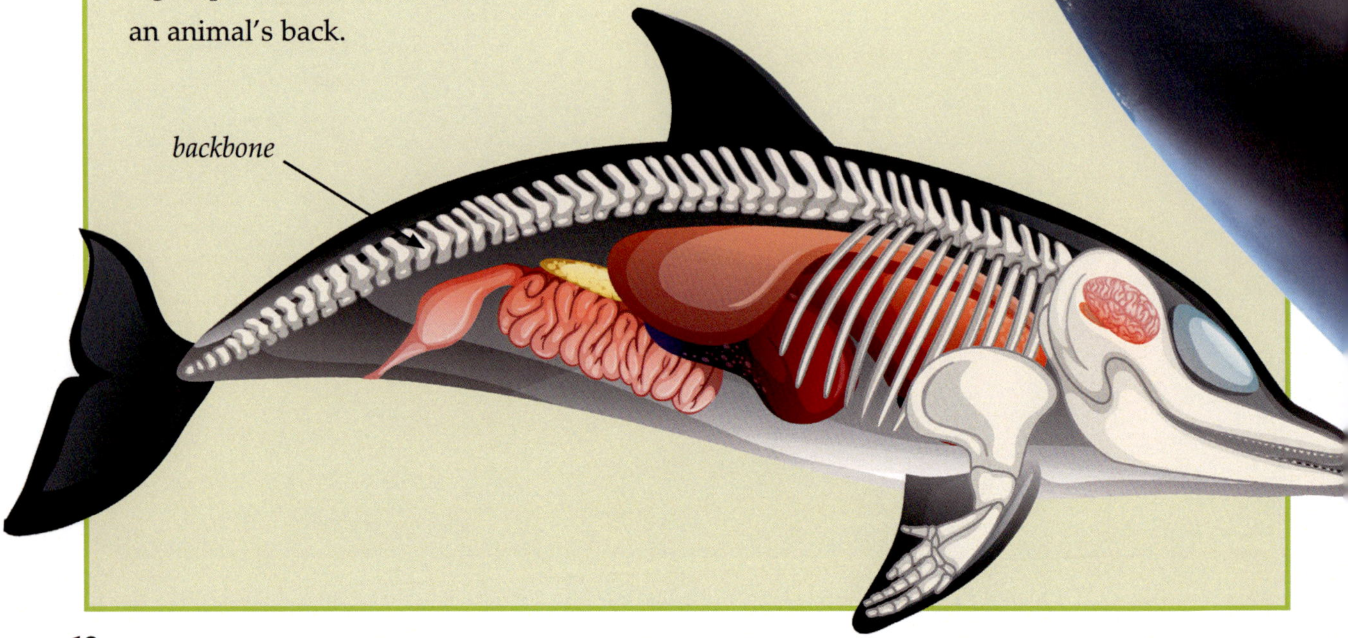

Polar bears look different from most marine mammals. They have strong legs for walking, running, and swimming. They have big paws. Having big paws keeps polar bears from sinking into snow.

Most marine mammals do not have eyelids. Instead, their eyes make oily tears. The tears protect each dolphin's eyes in water.

*Many marine mammals have **flippers**. Animals use their flippers to push themselves through water.*

Moms and babies

Marine mammal babies are **born**. Animals that are born are not inside eggs when they come out of the bodies of their mothers. Most marine mammal mothers care for their babies. They protect and feed the babies. The babies nurse, or drink milk from the bodies of their mothers.

In water, sea otter mothers carry their babies on their chests to keep the babies dry and warm.

This baby seal is nursing. Seal mothers nurse their babies until they are strong enough to swim on their own.

Born under water

Some marine mammal babies are born under water. Baby orcas are born under water. They know how to swim when they are born. They swim beside their mothers. Baby orcas like to play. This baby orca is jumping out of the water. Adult orcas sometimes play, too!

Born on land

Some marine mammal babies are born on land. Baby seals are born on land. Most mother seals care for their babies for only a short time. The babies care for themselves soon after they are born.

Finding food

Marine mammals find food in oceans. They eat a lot of food! Eating a lot of food adds blubber to their bodies. Most marine mammals are **carnivores**. Carnivores are animals that eat other animals. Marine mammals may eat krill, crabs, or fish. Some even eat other marine mammals!

Dolphins have many teeth. They use their teeth to catch fish.

A polar bear eats ringed seals. To catch a seal, the polar bear waits by a hole in the ice. When a seal sticks its head up through the hole, the polar bear grabs it.

Baleen whales

Baleen whales do not have teeth. Instead of teeth, they have **baleen plates**. To catch food, a baleen whale swims with its mouth open. Water and krill flow into its mouth. The whale then closes its mouth and pushes out the water. The krill get stuck in the baleen plates. The whale then swallows the krill.

baleen plates

krill

Eating plants

Manatees and dugongs are the only marine mammals that are **herbivores**. Herbivores are animals that eat only plants. Manatees and dugongs eat plants that grow on the bottom of oceans and rivers. This manatee is looking for some plants to eat.

Dolphins

Many kinds of marine mammals live in groups. Dolphins live in groups. Some dolphin groups are made up of only a few dolphins. Others are made up of hundreds of dolphins! Living in groups helps keep dolphins safe. Other animals find it more difficult to catch dolphins that are in a group.

The dolphins in a group often swim close together. They swim close enough to touch one another.

How do dolphins move?

Dolphins swim forward by moving their tails up and down. When a dolphin moves its tail up, the middle of its body bends down. When the dolphin moves its tail down, the middle of its body moves up.

Dolphins called whales

Some dolphins are called "whales," but they are actually dolphins! These dolphins are bigger than other dolphins are. They also look a lot like whales. Orcas are the biggest dolphins. They are often called "killer whales."

Porpoises

Porpoises are the smallest animals in their group. There are six kinds of porpoises. Most kinds of porpoises live alone. Other kinds sometimes live in small groups.

The porpoise below is a harbor porpoise. People know more about harbor porpoises than they do about other porpoises. Harbor porpoises live close to land, so it is easy for people to study them.

Porpoise or dolphin?

Porpoises and dolphins look a lot alike. They are different in many ways, however! The charts on this page will help you learn how porpoises and dolphins are different.

Porpoises

- Porpoises have rounded noses.
- Porpoises usually live alone.
- Porpoises find food alone.
- The bodies of porpoises are smaller than the bodies of dolphins.

porpoise

Dolphins

- The bodies of dolphins are larger than the bodies of porpoises.
- Most dolphins have pointed noses.
- Dolphins usually live in groups.
- Dolphins often find food in groups.

dolphin

Whale watching

Whales live in oceans all over the world. They are the largest ocean animals! Most whales are black, gray, or brown. The beluga whale is the only whale that is white. The whale on the left is a beluga whale. It is **spyhopping**. To spyhop, a whale holds its head above water and looks around.

The blue whale is the largest animal on Earth. One blue whale weighs more than what 30 elephants weigh!

Traveling whales

Some whales live in cold ocean waters. Many of these whales swim to warm waters in autumn. Whales, such as this humpback whale, swim to warm waters in autumn to have their babies. There are fewer animals in warmer waters that eat baby whales. The whales swim back to cold waters when their babies are older.

*Some whales have **barnacles** attached to their bodies. Barnacles are tiny living things. They feed on floating bits of food that the whales do not eat.*

Land lovers

Walruses, sea lions, and seals live mainly in oceans. They leave the water to rest on land. Seals also stay on land while they **molt**, or shed their fur. Seals molt once every year. Walruses, sea lions, and seals live in large groups on land. The animals in a group protect one another.

Walruses have two long teeth that stick out of their mouths. These teeth are called ***tusks****. Walruses use their tusks to protect themselves from other animals.*

"Walking" seals

Sea lions and some seals are **walking seals**. They can move easily in water and also on land. They turn their back flippers forward and "walk" on land using all four flippers. Walking seals have small **ear flaps** and long necks.

Crawling seals

Most seals are **crawling seals**. Crawling seals are good swimmers, but they cannot move easily on land. They use their front flippers to drag their bodies forward. Crawling seals do not have ear flaps. Their necks are shorter than the necks of walking seals.

Manatees and dugongs

Manatees and dugongs live only in warm shallow waters. Both these animals are slow swimmers. Manatees and dugongs swim to the bottom of the ocean to eat plants. They have many flat round teeth for chewing the plants.

This manatee is lifting its nose above water to breathe air.

So similar!

Can you tell which animal on this page is the manatee and which is the dugong? They look a lot alike! These pictures will help you learn how to tell these animals apart.

Manatees have rough skin.

Manatees have wide bodies.

Manatees have rounded tails.

The bodies of dugongs are narrower than the bodies of manatees are.

Dugongs have smooth skin.

Dugongs have tail flukes.

*Sea otters live together in groups called **rafts**.*

Sea otters

Sea otters are the only marine mammals that do not have blubber. The fur of these animals is thick enough to keep their bodies warm. Sea otters spend almost all their time in water. They usually float on their backs. They kick their back feet to move forward in the water.

This sea otter dove under the water to find food. It has found a crab to eat.

Polar bears

Polar bears live in cold places. They spend most of their time resting on huge pieces of ice that float in cold oceans. Some polar bears live in places where the ice melts in summer. During this time, these polar bears must live on land.

Polar bears are good swimmers.

Polar bears spend most of the day sleeping. This polar bear is living on land for the summer.

Warm blubber

Marine mammals spend a lot of time in chilly ocean waters. Do you remember how they keep warm? Most marine mammals have thick blubber on their bodies. How does blubber keep them warm? Try the experiment on the next page to learn how blubber works!

Dolphins do not have fur on their bodies. Blubber keeps them warm!

What you will need

To learn how blubber works, try some on!

To do this, you will need the following things:

- a bucket filled with cold water and ice cubes
- a pair of latex gloves
- some shortening
- a small plastic bag
- a strip of cloth or rope

Try on some blubber!

1. To begin, put on the latex gloves. Place your hand in the ice water. How does it feel?

2. Remove your hand from the water. Fill the small bag with shortening. Shortening is a type of fat, just like blubber.

3. Place your gloved hand in the bag of shortening. Use your other hand to push the shortening around until your whole hand is covered.

4. Ask a friend to tie the strip of cloth or rope around the top of the bag, with your hand still inside.

5. Stick your hand back into the ice water. Does it still feel cold? Why not? The layer of shortening is keeping you from feeling the cold water. A marine mammal's blubber works the same way.

Words to know and Index

Other index words